GOD OF OUR WEARY YEARS

GOD OF OUR WEARY YEARS

JEREMY ODOM

GOD OF OUR WEARY YEARS:
THE BLACK CHURCH AND THE UNCHANGING GOSPEL

Copyright © 2025 by Jeremy W Odom

All rights reserved.

No part of this book may be reproduced in any form without permission in writing from the publisher, except in the case of brief quotations embodied in critical articles or reviews.

The author has worked to ensure that all information in this book is accurate as of the time of publication. As research and practice advance, however, standards may change. For this reason, it is recommended that readers evaluate the applicability of any recommendations considering particular situations and changing standards.

iPreach Publications has made every effort to trace the ownership of all quotes. In the event of a question arising from the use of a quote, we regret any error made and will be pleased to make the necessary corrections in future printings and editions of this book.

ISBN 979-8-9914-9854-8

Library of Congress Control Number: 2025902111

All Scripture quotations, unless otherwise indicated, is taken from the *King James Version®* of the Bible. Public domain.

Printed in the United States of America

Contents

Dedication vi
Acknowledgements vii
Preface ix
Introduction xi

The Legacy of the Black Church 1
  1 The African Roots of Christianity 2
  2 The Black Church in Slavery and Reconstruction 7
  3 The Black Church and the Civil Rights Movement 13
What We Believe and Why It Matters 19
  4 The Unchanging Gospel 20
  5 Liberation Without Compromise 25
  6 Worship, Preaching, and the Spirit 31
Defending the Faith in a Changing World 35
  7 Answering the Critics 36
  8 The Black Church in a Digital Age 43
  9 Returning to Our First Love 48
Marching On Till Victory Is Won 54
  10 Marching On Till Victory Is Won 55

A Timeline of the Black Church's Historical Impact   61
Key Figures in Black Christian History   63
Suggested Books and Resources for Further Reading   66
Bibliography   69

DEDICATION

This book is dedicated to the members of the Saint Rest Baptist Church, whose faith and commitment continue to inspire me daily.

To my beloved nieces: Diamond Smith, Katelyn Smith, Destiny Smith, and A'Ziyah Armstrong. To my dear nephews: Kaunte West, Quintin West, Elton Smith, Jr., and Isaiah Armstrong. May this book serve as a legacy of faith and strength for generations to come.

To the esteemed brothers of the Most Worshipful Prince Hall Grand Lodge of Louisiana, under the leadership of Hon. Dr. A. Ralph Slaughter, Grand Master. To the dedicated sisters of Esther Grand Chapter Order of the Eastern Star, led by Sis. Elvera R. Shannon, Grand Worthy Matron, and Hon. Raywood T. Madison, Grand Worthy Patron. Your unwavering commitment to service and leadership is an inspiration.

Finally, I dedicate this work to the memories of the pioneers of the Civil Rights Movement—those who stood, marched, and sacrificed for justice and equality. Your legacy lives on in the continued fight for freedom and righteousness.

Acknowledgements

The journey of writing *God of Our Weary Years* has been one of faith, perseverance, and deep reflection. This work would not have been possible without the steadfast support, wisdom, and encouragement of many individuals who have shaped my understanding and conviction regarding the Black Church and its unchanging Gospel.

First and foremost, I give all honor and glory to God, who has guided me through this process, strengthening me at every step. His grace, wisdom, and sustaining power have been my anchor, and I pray that this work brings Him glory and edifies His people.

I extend my deepest gratitude to the members of Saint Rest Baptist Church, whose unwavering faith, love, and commitment to the work of the Lord continue to inspire me. Your dedication to the Gospel and service to the community embody the essence of the Black Church's mission. This book is, in many ways, a reflection of the faith you have lived and passed down through generations.

To my beloved family, your presence in my life has been a source of joy and strength. May you always walk in faith and never forget the rich legacy of those who came before you.

To the brothers of the Most Worshipful Prince Hall Grand Lodge of Louisiana, and to the sisters of Esther Grand Chapter Order of the Eastern Star, I extend my deepest appreciation. Your dedication to service, leadership, and the principles of faith and justice are invaluable to the community and have encouraged me greatly.

I also want to acknowledge and pay homage to the memory of the pioneers of the Civil Rights Movement, whose sacrifices paved the way for justice and equality. Their faith-driven courage reminds us that the Black Church has always been a catalyst for transformation and a beacon of hope in times of struggle.

A heartfelt thank you to my mentors, colleagues, and friends who have provided insight, guidance, and encouragement throughout this journey. Your support has strengthened my resolve to complete this work, and I am eternally grateful for your prayers and belief in the vision of this book.

I also wish to acknowledge the late Dr. Mallery Callahan, Sr., COL (R) Dr. Joseph F. Martin, Jr. USMC, MAJ (R) Dr. Solomon C. Shorter, Sr., Rev. George Stanley Lewis, Dea. James A. Dunn, SGM (R) David N. Moore, Daisy M. Jones, Dea. Clifford Blake, Sr., and the late Mr. Chris Payne, all of whom have greatly contributed to my appreciation and respect for African American history. Additionally, I honor the memory of the late Ben D. Johnson, Sr.

I also want to recognize Rev. James Graham, Mr. Marvin Blake, Jr., Chief Siggie Silvie, Chief Melvin Holmes, Mr. Thurman "Thunder" Miller, Sr., and Mr. Charlie Davis, Jr., whose dedication to preserving and sharing Black history has influenced my understanding and deepened my respect for our shared heritage.

Finally, to every reader—pastors, scholars, laypersons, and all who seek a deeper understanding of the Black Church and its enduring impact—may this book equip and inspire you. May you find in these pages a renewed faith in God, a deeper appreciation for the legacy of the Black Church, and a commitment to contend for the faith that has carried our people through weary years and silent tears.

To God be the glory for the things He has done.

Preface

For centuries, the Black Church has stood as a pillar of strength, a beacon of hope, and a refuge for the weary. It has been the heart of Black communities, a source of spiritual nourishment, and a force for justice and liberation. From the hush harbors of the enslaved to the grand sanctuaries of today, the Black Church has not only been a place of worship but also a catalyst for social change, a guardian of culture, and a steadfast proclaimer of the Gospel of Jesus Christ. Yet, as we journey further into the 21st century, the question arises: What is the future of the Black Church?

This book, *God of Our Weary Years: The Black Church and the Unchanging Gospel*, is an unapologetic affirmation of the Black Church's enduring mission. It is an exploration of its historical impact, theological foundations, and contemporary challenges. It is a call to remember, reclaim, and reinforce the unshakable truth that has carried the Black Church through oppression, struggle, and triumph—the truth of the Gospel.

This work is not merely an academic endeavor but a deeply personal reflection on the significance of the Black Church in shaping my own faith and convictions. Growing up in the Black Church, I witnessed firsthand its power to transform lives, to equip believers for service, and to inspire resistance against injustice. It was in the sanctuary of the Black Church that I learned to pray, to sing songs of Zion, and to trust in the unchanging God who has sustained our people through weary years and silent tears. It is this faith—the faith of our ancestors—that must remain central as the Black Church moves forward.

However, we must also acknowledge that the Black Church stands at a crossroads. The rise of secularism, the exodus of younger generations from organized religion, the infiltration of diluted theology, and the growing appeal of alternative Black spiritual movements all challenge the Church's future. Some have questioned whether the Black Church still matters, whether its voice still carries the prophetic power it once did. This book contends that it does, and it must.

Through biblical exposition, historical analysis, and cultural critique, *God of Our Weary Years* seeks to reaffirm that the Black Church is not merely a cultural institution—it is the living body of Christ. It is called not to conform to the shifting tides of society but to remain steadfast in its proclamation of the unchanging Gospel. The same faith that sustained our ancestors remains our source of strength today. The same God who guided Harriet Tubman, Richard Allen, Nat Turner, and Martin Luther King Jr. is still moving among His people, calling us to faithfulness, justice, and discipleship.

As you journey through these pages, my hope is that you will be both challenged and encouraged. Whether you are a pastor, a scholar, a layperson, or someone seeking a deeper understanding of the Black Church's role in faith and history, I pray that this book will stir within you a renewed commitment to contending for the faith. May it inspire you to honor the past, engage the present, and prepare for the future with conviction and courage.

The Black Church has marched through centuries of trials and triumphs, but our work is not yet finished. We press on, we persevere, and we stand firm in the Gospel that has never failed us. To the weary, the hopeful, the faithful, and the searching—this book is for you.

To God be the glory.
JEREMY W. ODOM
FEB 2025

Introduction

Throughout history, the Black Church has stood as a pillar of faith, resilience, and hope for generations. Born out of struggle yet anchored in unwavering belief, it has been more than just a place of worship—it has been a sanctuary of liberation, a stronghold of justice, and a voice for the voiceless. Despite the shifting tides of history and the evolving challenges faced by African Americans, one thing remains unchanged: the Gospel of Jesus Christ.

The title of this book, *God of Our Weary Years: The Black Church and the Unchanging Gospel*, is inspired by the powerful words of James Weldon Johnson's hymn, *Lift Every Voice and Sing*. The phrase 'God of our weary years' speaks to the enduring faith of Black people, a faith that has carried us through the darkest valleys of slavery, segregation, systemic injustice, and cultural marginalization. In every generation, the Black Church has served as both a lighthouse guiding its people to spiritual truth and a fortress against the storms of oppression.

Yet today, the Black Church stands at a crossroads. We find ourselves contending with modern challenges that threaten to erode the foundation upon which our faith has stood. A rising tide of skepticism, fueled by claims that Christianity is a tool of oppression, has led some to abandon the faith of their ancestors. The influence of secular movements, alternative spiritualities, and a shifting cultural landscape has caused many to question whether the message of Christ is still relevant to Black lives today.

This book seeks to affirm what history has already proven: the Gospel is not a relic of the past but a living, breathing truth that has sustained our people for centuries. Christianity is not the 'white man's religion'—it is a faith deeply embedded in the African story, dating back to the earliest days of the Church. The Black Church has been a central force in shaping both theology and social change, serving as the heartbeat of our communities. This book will explore how the faith that strengthened our ancestors is still the faith that will guide us today.

In these pages, we will take a journey through the history, theology, and apologetics of the Black Church. We will examine the African roots of Christianity, the role of faith in the struggle for freedom, and the biblical truths that have upheld our churches for generations. We will also confront the rising skepticism of the digital age, addressing misconceptions and reclaiming the Black Church's theological legacy.

As we embark on this journey together, my prayer is that this book will serve as a reaffirmation of our spiritual heritage and a call to stand firm in the unchanging Gospel. The God of our weary years is still the God of today, and the faith that brought us through will continue to sustain us for generations to come.

Let us press on, lifting every voice in testimony, and march on till victory is won.

The Legacy of the
Black Church

1

The African Roots of Christianity

Christianity did not arrive in Africa through European colonization; rather, it has deep and ancient roots on the continent. Long before the transatlantic slave trade, before European missionaries set foot on African soil, and even before Christianity spread widely throughout Europe, Africans were already a part of the Christian faith.

This chapter seeks to dismantle the common misconception that Christianity is a "white man's religion" by tracing its presence in Africa back to the first century. We will explore biblical references, historical evidence, and the contributions of African theologians who shaped Christian doctrine.

Historical Presence of Christianity in Africa

Biblical Evidence of Christianity in Africa

Christianity's connection to Africa is evident in both the Old and New Testaments. One of the most significant biblical references to Christianity's African roots is the story of the Ethiopian eunuch in

Acts 8:26-39. This passage describes an official from Ethiopia, a high-ranking figure in Queen Candace's court, encountering Philip the Evangelist. The Ethiopian had been reading from Isaiah's prophecy but lacked understanding until Philip explained how it pointed to Jesus Christ. After receiving the explanation, the Ethiopian eagerly requested baptism, making him one of the earliest recorded converts to Christianity. His return to Ethiopia likely helped introduce the Gospel to the region, demonstrating that Africa's engagement with Christianity predates European expansion.

The Old Testament also speaks of Africa in various prophetic and historical contexts. Zephaniah 3:10 (KJV) states, *"From beyond the rivers of Ethiopia my suppliants, even the daughter of my dispersed, shall bring mine offering."* This verse highlights Ethiopia as a region connected to God's plan for worshippers. Additionally, Psalm 68:31 (KJV) declares, *"Princes shall come out of Egypt; Ethiopia shall soon stretch out her hands unto God."* Such passages indicate that Africans were part of God's divine narrative long before modern missionary efforts.

Christianity in North Africa: The Early Church Fathers

North Africa played a pivotal role in shaping Christian thought and theology, producing some of the most influential theologians of early Christianity.

Tertullian (c. 160-220 AD), an early Christian apologist from Carthage (modern-day Tunisia), is credited with coining the term "Trinity." His works defended the faith against Roman persecution and heretical movements, laying the groundwork for Latin Christian theology. His influence extended beyond Africa, shaping doctrinal debates in the broader Christian world.

Origen (c. 185-254 AD) of Alexandria was one of the most prolific theologians of the early church. Known for his extensive biblical commentaries, Origen emphasized allegorical interpretation of Scripture, which influenced Christian hermeneutics for centuries. He also formulated significant theological ideas, such as the preexistence of souls and the importance of moral purity in Christian life.

Athanasius (c. 296-373 AD), another African theologian, was central in defending the doctrine of the Trinity against Arianism. As Bishop of Alexandria, he was instrumental in shaping the Nicene Creed, a foundational statement of Christian belief that continues to be affirmed by churches worldwide. His tenacity in standing against heresy earned him the title "Athanasius Contra Mundum" (Athanasius Against the World).

Augustine of Hippo (354-430 AD) is arguably the most influential African theologian in Christian history. His works, including *Confessions* and *The City of God*, are cornerstones of Christian philosophy and doctrine. Augustine's theology on grace, predestination, and original sin shaped Western Christianity, and his intellectual legacy remains a dominant force in theological study today.

The Misconception of Christianity as a European Religion

Despite Africa's deep-rooted connection to Christianity, colonial and enslaver narratives distorted the perception of the faith. The transatlantic slave trade and European imperialism attempted to rebrand Christianity as a tool of subjugation rather than liberation. However, historical records show that African Christians long predated European involvement in spreading the Gospel.

The **Coptic Orthodox Church in Egypt** and the **Ethiopian Orthodox Church** are among the oldest Christian traditions in the world, maintaining unbroken theological and liturgical traditions from the early centuries of Christianity.

Apologetic Defense: Answering the Critics

Critics often claim that Christianity was imposed upon Africans by European colonizers, erasing their indigenous spiritual traditions. However, this perspective fails to acknowledge that Christianity was well established in Africa long before colonial rule. African Christians existed in Egypt, Ethiopia, and North Africa for centuries before European nations became dominant Christian powers. The presence of early African theologians, martyrs, and churches proves that Christianity was not an external imposition but an internal development within the continent itself.

Another common argument against Christianity in the Black community is that it was used as a tool for oppression. It is true that some enslavers manipulated biblical passages to justify slavery, but this does not mean that Christianity itself is an oppressive faith. In fact, many Black Christians, both enslaved and free, found liberation and strength in the Bible's teachings. Figures such as Harriet Tubman and Frederick Douglass drew from Christian theology to fuel their resistance against oppression, demonstrating that Christianity, when properly understood, serves as a source of empowerment rather than enslavement.

A third criticism is that African spirituality is the true, untainted heritage of Black people, and Christianity represents a foreign intrusion. While traditional African religions are indeed part of the continent's cultural history, the argument that Christianity is wholly foreign ignores the fact that African communities have played a vital role in Christian history. From the Ethiopian Orthodox Church's centuries-long existence to the presence of African theologians in shaping church doctrine, Africa's contributions to Christianity are undeniable. The assertion that Christianity is "un-African" disregards these historical realities and perpetuates a false narrative.

Conclusion: Reclaiming the Black Church's Historical Identity

Understanding the African roots of Christianity allows us to reclaim our rightful place in biblical and church history. The faith that has sustained Black people through slavery, segregation, and systemic injustice is the same faith that empowered early African Christians to shape global Christianity.

As we move forward, let us do so with the assurance that our faith is not borrowed—it is inherited. Christianity belongs to us as much as it does to any other people group, and its power continues to transform lives today.

The God of our weary years is the same God of our African ancestors, and He remains unchanging in His faithfulness to His people.

2

The Black Church in Slavery and Reconstruction

The Black Church was not merely a product of oppression but a force of resistance, hope, and liberation. During the era of slavery and the turbulent years of Reconstruction, Christianity became a cornerstone for enslaved Africans, providing spiritual strength and a vision for freedom.

It was in the secret prayer meetings, the sorrow songs, and the preached Word that Black believers found hope in a God who liberates. While their oppressors manipulated Scripture to justify their subjugation, the enslaved discovered a different God—a God who parted the Red Sea, who heard the cries of the oppressed, and who promised ultimate deliverance.

This chapter explores how the Black Church emerged during slavery and Reconstruction, its theological foundation, and how it became the leading institution in shaping Black identity and advocacy for justice.

Historical Development of the Black Church During Slavery

Biblical Evidence of God's Deliverance in Times of Oppression

The enslaved Africans saw their plight reflected in the biblical stories of captivity and deliverance. Exodus 3:7-8 (KJV) reads: *"And the Lord said, I have surely seen the affliction of my people which are in Egypt, and have heard their cry by reason of their taskmasters; for I know their sorrows; And I am come down to deliver them out of the hand of the Egyptians."* The story of the Israelites' deliverance became a central narrative in Black spiritual life, reinforcing the belief that God was on the side of the oppressed.

Similarly, Luke 4:18-19 (KJV) records Jesus declaring: *"The Spirit of the Lord is upon me, because he hath anointed me to preach the gospel to the poor; he hath sent me to heal the brokenhearted, to preach deliverance to the captives, and recovering of sight to the blind, to set at liberty them that are bruised, To preach the acceptable year of the Lord."* This passage assured enslaved Christians that their suffering was not unseen and that Christ Himself came to bring freedom, both spiritually and physically.

The Underground Church and Slave Christianity

The Black Church was born in the hush harbors—secret gathering places where enslaved people worshiped away from the eyes of their masters. These meetings were necessary because plantation owners feared that Christianity, when rightly understood, would inspire rebellion.

In the hush harbors, enslaved preachers reinterpreted the Scriptures beyond the slaveholder's distortions. While slaveowners emphasized texts like *"Servants, be obedient to them that are your masters according to the flesh"* (Ephesians 6:5, KJV), Black believers clung to the Exodus story and the promise of Jesus' return. Their faith was forged in hardship, yet it remained defiant, birthing spirituals that spoke of freedom in both this world and the next.

The Role of the Black Church During Reconstruction

Rebuilding Faith and Community

Following Emancipation, newly freed Black people saw the church as more than a house of worship—it was the center of community rebuilding. The church provided schooling, economic support, and leadership training. It was during this period that many historically Black denominations, such as the African Methodist Episcopal (AME) Church and the National Baptist Convention, saw rapid growth.

Many of the first schools for freed slaves were founded by Black churches and clergy. Institutions like Howard University, Fisk University, and Morehouse College had direct ties to church leadership, emphasizing not only religious education but also general literacy and vocational training. The belief was that education and faith went hand in hand, enabling formerly enslaved people to chart new paths for themselves and future generations.

Black churches also became economic hubs. Many congregations formed mutual aid societies, where members pooled resources to help those in financial need. Whether through land ownership cooperatives or providing shelter for the homeless, the Black Church extended its influence beyond the pulpit and into daily survival and progress.

Additionally, the Black Church provided an emotional and psychological refuge. Having endured the trauma of slavery, many African Americans found solace in the communal worship experience, which reinforced their dignity and worth. The church's music, prayers, and rituals helped to heal wounds inflicted by oppression and to instill hope for a better future.

Church Leaders as Social and Political Advocates

Black clergy became the primary spokesmen for their communities. Men like Henry McNeal Turner of the AME Church preached a message of self-determination, telling Black people that they had the same God-given rights as whites. Clergy played a vital role in organizing freedmen's schools, advocating for voting rights, and resisting the new forms of oppression that arose under Jim Crow laws.

Many Black pastors became actively involved in politics. Some ran for office themselves, while others encouraged voter registration and civic engagement. Churches became meeting places for political strategy, organizing rallies, and mobilizing communities to push for legal and civil rights. Ministers such as Richard Allen and Frederick Douglass used their pulpits as platforms to speak against racial injustice, urging their congregations to engage in activism.

Additionally, Black women in the church also played significant roles. Figures like Sojourner Truth and Harriet Tubman used Christian doctrine to challenge societal norms and advocate for equal rights. Women organized missionary societies, literacy programs, and relief efforts, ensuring that Black communities could survive and thrive under hostile conditions.

The church also helped sustain the fight against racial violence. In response to the rise of the Ku Klux Klan and other white supremacist groups, churches functioned as safe havens where community members could seek protection and plan strategies to counteract terror. Clergy and congregants alike worked to establish security networks, advocating self-defense while maintaining a message of faith and perseverance.

Apologetic Defense: Answering the Critics

Critics argue that Christianity was simply a tool of oppression, imposed upon enslaved Africans to keep them subservient. While it is true that slaveholders twisted Scripture for their benefit, this does not mean that Christianity itself was an oppressive faith. Instead, it became a faith of resilience and defiance. Enslaved Africans identified more with the suffering of Christ than with the power of their oppressors, finding in the Gospel the ultimate assurance of justice and liberation.

A second criticism is that the Black Church was passive in the fight for freedom, focusing only on heaven rather than earthly liberation. However, history disproves this claim. Many slave revolts, including those led by Nat Turner and Denmark Vesey, were directly influenced by biblical interpretations of justice. The Black Church was not an idle institution; it was the heartbeat of resistance.

A third argument posits that Black people should abandon Christianity altogether in favor of African spiritual traditions. While honoring African heritage is vital, it is inaccurate to suggest that Christianity is foreign to Black identity. As we saw in Chapter 1, African Christians were among the earliest followers of Christ. The faith that sustained our ancestors was not a borrowed faith but a faith of their own discovery, interpretation, and liberation.

Conclusion: The Church as a Vehicle of Freedom

The Black Church, born in the fires of slavery and Reconstruction, has never been merely a religious institution. It has been a force for justice, a sanctuary for the weary, and a prophetic voice calling for the liberation of all people. While oppressors tried to use the Gospel to chain them, enslaved Africans saw in it the promise of freedom. The God who brought Israel out of Egypt was the same God who walked with them through slavery, Reconstruction, and beyond.

As we continue this journey, we must recognize that the Black Church is not just a historical artifact but a living testament to faith in the midst of suffering. The God of our weary years remains with us, guiding us toward justice, righteousness, and ultimate liberation.

3

The Black Church and the Civil Rights Movement

The Civil Rights Movement of the mid-20th century was not merely a political or social revolution—it was a theological movement deeply rooted in the Black Church. Faith leaders, congregations, and Christian doctrine played a central role in shaping the strategies, ideologies, and perseverance of the movement.

This chapter will explore how the Black Church became the epicenter of the Civil Rights Movement, how biblical principles influenced the fight for justice, and how leaders like Martin Luther King Jr., Fannie Lou Hamer, and James Cone used theology as a framework for activism.

Theological Foundations of the Civil Rights Movement

Biblical Justification for Justice and Liberation

Throughout history, the Black Church interpreted Scripture as a divine mandate for justice and social action. Micah 6:8 (KJV) states, *"He hath shewed thee, O man, what is good; and what doth the Lord require of thee, but to do justly, and to love mercy, and to walk humbly with thy*

God?" This passage became a theological cornerstone for activists seeking biblical justification for their resistance to oppression.

Luke 4:18-19 (KJV) also played a significant role in civil rights theology: *"The Spirit of the Lord is upon me, because he hath anointed me to preach the gospel to the poor; he hath sent me to heal the brokenhearted, to preach deliverance to the captives, and recovering of sight to the blind, to set at liberty them that are bruised."* This verse, often cited by Martin Luther King Jr., reinforced the belief that Christ Himself was concerned with the liberation of the oppressed.

The Social Gospel and Liberation Theology

The Social Gospel movement emerged in the late 19th and early 20th centuries, advocating that Christian faith should address social injustices such as poverty, racial inequality, and economic exploitation. The movement taught that salvation was not only a spiritual matter but also involved the transformation of society. Many Black churches adopted this approach, seeing the fight against segregation and oppression as a direct extension of their Christian duty.

Liberation Theology, popularized in the mid-20th century, further developed the idea that God sides with the oppressed. James Cone, a pioneering theologian of Black Liberation Theology, argued that the Gospel of Christ demanded action against systemic oppression. He contended that Jesus was not merely a passive savior but a revolutionary figure advocating for justice. Cone's writings challenged the white American church's silence on racial injustice and called for a faith that engaged directly with social realities. His works emphasized that Christianity was a means of empowerment, where faith in Christ gave believers the strength to resist dehumanization and strive for equality.

Together, the Social Gospel and Liberation Theology provided an intellectual and theological foundation for civil rights activists. They inspired church leaders to see the movement as a divine mission rather than just a political effort. These theological frameworks reinforced the belief that justice, love, and righteousness were inseparable from Christian discipleship.

The Role of the Black Church in Organizing the Movement

Churches as Meeting Halls and Mobilization Centers

The Black Church served as more than a house of worship; it was the organizational hub of the Civil Rights Movement. Churches hosted strategy meetings, trained activists, and provided safe spaces for freedom fighters.

The Montgomery Bus Boycott (1955-1956) began in Black churches, with preachers like Martin Luther King Jr. delivering sermons that inspired mass participation. Similarly, the Southern Christian Leadership Conference (SCLC) was founded in 1957 as a coalition of Black churches committed to nonviolent resistance.

Clergy as Movement Leaders

Many key civil rights leaders were clergy members who framed the struggle for racial justice as a divine calling. Dr. Martin Luther King Jr., a Baptist minister, championed nonviolent resistance, drawing inspiration from Jesus' Sermon on the Mount (Matthew 5-7, KJV) and the philosophy of Mahatma Gandhi. His speeches and writings reflected a deep commitment to biblical justice, challenging both the American government and the white church to align themselves with righteousness.

Fannie Lou Hamer, a deaconess and activist, exemplified faith-based activism. Her famous declaration, *"I'm sick and tired of being sick and tired,"* was grounded in her conviction that God demanded justice. Hamer's unwavering faith gave her the strength to fight for voting rights despite enduring violent opposition.

Rev. Fred Shuttlesworth, a fiery preacher in Birmingham, Alabama, fearlessly led desegregation efforts, surviving bombings and physical attacks while advocating for change. His church served as a base for activism, demonstrating how deeply entwined faith and resistance were during the movement.

The Black Church and the Power of Worship in Protest

Gospel Music as a Tool of Resistance

Gospel music played a crucial role in the Civil Rights Movement, serving as both an emotional anchor and a form of protest. Songs like *"We Shall Overcome"* and *"Ain't Gonna Let Nobody Turn Me Around"* were not just melodies; they were theological affirmations of perseverance and hope. These songs originated in the Black Church and were often sung during marches, mass meetings, and sit-ins, reinforcing the spiritual and communal unity of the movement.

Music acted as an emotional and psychological refuge, giving activists the courage to face violent opposition. The rhythms and lyrics carried biblical themes of deliverance, much like the spirituals sung by enslaved ancestors. Gospel music was not just entertainment—it was resistance.

Prayer and Spiritual Endurance

Prayer was a sustaining force for the movement. Before embarking on marches or demonstrations, activists gathered in churches to pray, seeking divine strength and protection. Prayer meetings functioned as spiritual fortification, reminding participants that their struggle was not merely against human laws but against deeper, systemic injustices.

Many civil rights leaders testified that their personal faith helped them endure threats, imprisonment, and violence. Their belief in a just God gave them the resilience to continue, even when the odds seemed insurmountable. Prayer was an act of faith and defiance, reinforcing the certainty that justice would ultimately prevail.

Apologetic Defense: Answering the Critics
Critics of the Civil Rights Movement, both then and now, have attempted to challenge the role of Christianity in the fight for racial justice. Some argue that Christianity is not inherently a faith of liberation, citing its historical misuse to justify slavery and segregation. While it is true that many white churches upheld racist ideologies, the Black Church reclaimed Christianity as a force for justice. The biblical narrative, from the Exodus to the teachings of Jesus, is filled with messages of deliverance, making it a natural foundation for civil rights activism.

Another criticism suggests that the Black Church should have remained focused solely on spiritual matters rather than engaging in activism. However, this perspective ignores the biblical mandate for justice. Prophets such as Amos and Isaiah spoke against corrupt rulers, and Jesus Himself challenged oppressive systems. The Civil Rights Movement was a continuation of this tradition.

A final criticism questions the effectiveness of nonviolent resistance, arguing that it was too passive. However, nonviolence was both a moral and strategic choice. Rooted in Christian teachings, it exposed the brutality of white supremacist systems, garnering national and global sympathy for the movement. The Black Church's commitment to nonviolence demonstrated the power of faith-driven resistance.

Conclusion: The Enduring Legacy of the Black Church in Activism

The Civil Rights Movement did not end in the 1960s—it continues in modern struggles for racial and economic justice. The Black Church remains a critical institution in shaping moral leadership and mobilizing communities against systemic injustice.

The God of our weary years, the God of our silent tears, still calls His people to righteousness, mercy, and action.

What We Believe and Why It Matters

4

The Unchanging Gospel

The strength of the Black Church lies in its unwavering commitment to the Gospel of Jesus Christ. Throughout history, the Black Church has faced oppression, discrimination, and cultural shifts, yet it has remained steadfast in preaching salvation, redemption, and the transformative power of God's Word. While societal challenges have evolved, the Gospel message has not changed. The faith that sustained enslaved Africans, empowered civil rights activists, and nurtured generations of Black believers remains just as relevant today.

This chapter will explore the core doctrinal tenets of the Black Church, examining how it has upheld biblical truths despite external pressures. We will highlight the essential teachings of salvation, faith, and the role of the Holy Spirit, and we will address challenges that have sought to dilute or redefine the Gospel message.

The Core Doctrines of the Black Church

The Authority of Scripture
From its inception, the Black Church has upheld the Bible as the ultimate authority on faith and life. The words of 2 Timothy 3:16-17 (KJV) affirm this stance: *"All scripture is given by inspiration of God, and*

is profitable for doctrine, for reproof, for correction, for instruction in righteousness: That the man of God may be perfect, thoroughly furnished unto all good works." The Bible has served as both a source of comfort and a foundation for social justice, guiding believers through slavery, segregation, and ongoing struggles for equality.

The authority of Scripture is what enabled the Black Church to resist cultural oppression and hold onto a faith that others attempted to distort. By interpreting the Bible through the lens of liberation and divine justice, Black believers found in Scripture a call to persevere, to fight for righteousness, and to trust in God's promises. The unwavering belief in biblical authority has safeguarded the Black Church against theological compromise and secular reinterpretation.

Salvation Through Jesus Christ

The Black Church has consistently preached that salvation comes through Jesus Christ alone. Acts 4:12 (KJV) states, *"Neither is there salvation in any other: for there is none other name under heaven given among men, whereby we must be saved."* This message of redemption has been a pillar of Black Christian identity, affirming that freedom is not only a physical pursuit but a spiritual reality secured through faith in Christ.

For generations, this doctrine has remained the foundation of Black preaching and evangelism. Amid systemic injustices, the promise of eternal salvation has provided hope beyond present suffering. The Black Church has always emphasized that Jesus' redemptive power is available to all, regardless of status, race, or earthly circumstance.

The Role of the Holy Spirit

The Holy Spirit has played a dynamic role in shaping Black worship, preaching, and community engagement. From traditional call-and-response worship to Spirit-filled revivals, the Black Church has always emphasized the active presence of the Holy Spirit. John 14:26 (KJV) declares, *"But the Comforter, which is the Holy Ghost, whom the Father will send in my name, he shall teach you all things, and bring all things to your remembrance, whatsoever I have said unto you."* The Spirit's guidance has been essential in leading the Black Church through difficult times and inspiring resilience.

The power of the Holy Spirit manifests in the passionate and deeply expressive worship style of the Black Church. It fuels prayer meetings, anoints preachers, and provides believers with supernatural strength to endure trials. The Spirit's role in both personal transformation and communal revival cannot be overstated; it is the sustaining force that has kept the Black Church vibrant and mission-driven.

Challenges to the Gospel in the Modern Era

Cultural Relativism and Secularism

In an age of increasing secularization, some have attempted to redefine Christianity to fit contemporary social norms. The Black Church has faced pressures to compromise biblical truths in favor of cultural acceptance. However, Romans 12:2 (KJV) warns against conforming to the world: *"And be not conformed to this world: but be ye transformed by the renewing of your mind, that ye may prove what is that good, and acceptable, and perfect, will of God."* The call to uphold the unchanging Gospel remains urgent in a world that often seeks to dilute its message.

This challenge is particularly relevant in discussions on morality, sexuality, and ethical living. The Black Church must stand firm on Scripture while navigating these societal pressures with wisdom and love.

Prosperity Gospel and False Teachings

The rise of the prosperity gospel has posed a theological challenge to the Black Church. While biblical prosperity encompasses spiritual and material well-being, some distortions have led to a focus on wealth over holiness. 1 Timothy 6:10 (KJV) warns, *"For the love of money is the root of all evil."* The true Gospel calls believers to seek first the kingdom of God rather than worldly riches.

The false teaching that equates material success with divine favor has misled many. The Black Church, historically rooted in the message of hope and perseverance, must continue to reject any doctrine that undermines the true cost of discipleship and promotes selfish gain over godly character.

The Enduring Power of the Gospel

Despite the challenges, the Gospel remains the foundation of the Black Church. It has sustained communities, fostered resilience, and empowered believers to face adversity with faith. Hebrews 13:8 (KJV) affirms, *"Jesus Christ the same yesterday, and today, and forever."* The unchanging nature of Christ reassures believers that the faith of our forebears is still relevant and powerful today.

The enduring power of the Gospel is evident in how it continues to shape lives, inspire movements, and bring transformation to individuals and communities. It has withstood slavery, segregation, and systemic racism, proving time and again that the Word of God prevails over all human opposition.

Apologetic Defense: Answering the Critics

Critics argue that the Black Church is resistant to modern progress and too rigid in its adherence to biblical doctrine. However, this perspective fails to recognize that the Black Church has always been progressive in the truest sense—pushing forward justice, equity, and righteousness under the authority of Scripture. The message of Christ transcends cultural trends and remains the guiding light for moral and spiritual progress.

Some also claim that the Black Church's commitment to social justice undermines its spiritual mission. In response, we must remember that Christ Himself preached justice and righteousness. The Black Church does not have to choose between faith and activism; rather, it must ensure that its activism is biblically rooted and theologically sound.

Conclusion

The Black Church stands as a testament to the endurance of the Gospel. Through trials and triumphs, it has upheld the message of Jesus Christ with unwavering faith. As new generations navigate evolving cultural landscapes, the call remains the same—to preach the Gospel, stand firm on biblical truth, and continue the legacy of faith that has carried the Black Church through centuries. The God of our weary years and silent tears remains ever-present, guiding His people with an unchanging Gospel.

5

Liberation Without Compromise

The Black Church has long been a prophetic voice in the fight for justice, deeply rooted in the biblical call to righteousness. While many institutions have faltered in the face of oppression, the Black Church has historically balanced faith and activism, advocating for justice without compromising the Gospel.

This chapter will explore the biblical foundation for justice, how the Black Church has effectively maintained a balance between faith and social activism, and the dangers of distorting the Gospel for political or ideological movements. True liberation comes not from human efforts alone but through a commitment to God's divine standard of righteousness.

The Biblical Call for Justice

Micah 6:8 (KJV) serves as one of the clearest biblical mandates for justice: *"He hath shewed thee, O man, what is good; and what doth the Lord require of thee, but to do justly, and to love mercy, and to walk humbly with thy God?"* This verse encapsulates the divine expectation that justice is not optional for believers but a requirement of faithful living.

Throughout Scripture, justice and righteousness are inseparable. Isaiah 1:17 (KJV) commands, *"Learn to do well; seek judgment, relieve the oppressed, judge the fatherless, plead for the widow."* Proverbs 21:3 (KJV) reinforces this principle: *"To do justice and judgment is more acceptable to the Lord than sacrifice."* These verses illustrate that justice is not merely a social concern but a reflection of God's moral order.

For centuries, the Black Church has been a faithful steward of this biblical mandate, advocating for the poor, fighting against systemic injustice, and holding society accountable to God's righteous standards. The Civil Rights Movement, led by clergy such as Dr. Martin Luther King Jr., exemplified how justice and righteousness must go hand in hand to effect real change.

How the Black Church Balances Faith and Activism

The ability of the Black Church to balance faith and activism stems from a deep understanding that social justice and the Gospel are not mutually exclusive. Rather, they are intricately connected. From the days of slavery to the Civil Rights Movement and beyond, the Black Church has been at the forefront of advocating for justice while remaining steadfast in its commitment to biblical truth.

Biblical activism within the Black Church has always been guided by Scripture. Leaders and congregants alike have drawn upon the prophetic tradition of the Bible, viewing their work for justice as an extension of God's kingdom on earth. The Exodus narrative, in which God delivers the Israelites from bondage, has served as a guiding theological framework for Black liberation theology. The belief that God hears the cries of the oppressed has fueled the Church's advocacy efforts, ensuring that faith remains central to the fight for justice.

At the same time, the Black Church has sought to uphold moral integrity in its advocacy. While many social movements rise and fall, the Church's commitment to justice has remained grounded in the eternal truths of Scripture. This means rejecting ideologies that seek justice without righteousness and ensuring that activism does not lead to theological compromise. True justice, according to biblical teaching, must reflect God's righteousness and cannot be defined solely by political ideologies or shifting cultural trends.

Another key aspect of the Black Church's balance is its role as a prophetic voice rather than a political tool. Historically, the Church has resisted being co-opted by partisan politics, choosing instead to speak truth to power regardless of political affiliation. This has allowed it to remain an independent force for justice, holding both secular and religious institutions accountable without compromising its spiritual mission. By anchoring activism in faith and remaining rooted in the Word of God, the Black Church has been able to navigate the complexities of justice work while maintaining its theological integrity. The ability of the Black Church to balance faith and activism stems from a deep understanding that social justice and the Gospel are not mutually exclusive. Rather, they are intricately connected.

The Dangers of Distorting the Gospel for Social Movements

While the call for justice is clear in Scripture, history has shown the dangers of distorting the Gospel to fit secular movements. Without a foundation in biblical truth, justice efforts can become disconnected from their divine purpose and susceptible to theological compromise. The Black Church must remain vigilant in ensuring that its pursuit of justice does not lead to a dilution of the Gospel message.

One significant danger is the temptation to redefine biblical justice through a purely secular lens. When justice is detached from God's moral law, it risks becoming moral relativism, where truth is subjective and ever-changing. This can lead to movements that, while well-intentioned, lack the grounding necessary to create lasting and meaningful change. True justice is rooted in the character of God, and efforts to seek justice must be aligned with His divine standards rather than human philosophies.

Another challenge is the elevation of activism over the Gospel. While advocating for social change is essential, it should never overshadow the Church's primary mission: to preach the Gospel and lead souls to Christ. Activism that is detached from the message of salvation loses its eternal significance. The Black Church has historically understood this balance, ensuring that the pursuit of justice does not replace the ultimate goal of spiritual transformation.

Additionally, justice efforts that become overly politicized can create division within the Church. When justice is framed primarily through the lens of political ideology rather than biblical truth, it can fracture congregations and distract from the Church's central mission. The Black Church must remain unified in its commitment to both faith and justice, ensuring that its advocacy is guided by Scripture rather than external pressures.

To remain faithful to its calling, the Black Church must uphold a vision of justice that is both biblically sound and socially transformative. By keeping Christ at the center, the Church can continue to be a beacon of hope, righteousness, and liberation without compromising the integrity of the Gospel. While the call for justice is clear in Scripture, history has shown the dangers of distorting the Gospel to fit secular movements. Without a foundation in biblical truth, justice efforts can become disconnected from their divine purpose.

Apologetic Defense: Answering the Critics

Critics argue that the Black Church should focus solely on spiritual matters and avoid involvement in social issues. However, this argument misrepresents both Scripture and history. The prophets of the Old Testament, Jesus Himself, and the apostles all spoke against oppression and injustice.

Some claim that engaging in social justice is a distraction from the Gospel. In response, we affirm that justice is not separate from the Gospel but an essential part of living out our faith. As James 2:26 (KJV) states, *"For as the body without the spirit is dead, so faith without works is dead also."* Faith that does not seek justice is incomplete.

Others suggest that justice is inherently a secular concern. Yet, the Bible consistently portrays God as a defender of the oppressed. The Black Church's involvement in justice movements is not a deviation from biblical faith but an embodiment of it.

Conclusion

Liberation without compromise requires that the Black Church remain steadfast in its theological convictions while continuing to advocate for justice. The call of Micah 6:8 remains as relevant today as it was in biblical times—believers must do justly, love mercy, and walk humbly with God.

The Black Church has a divine mandate to be both a spiritual sanctuary and a voice for righteousness in society. However, it must never allow secular ideologies to overshadow its core mission: proclaiming the unchanging Gospel of Jesus Christ. Justice that is not grounded in the truth of God's Word will ultimately fail, but when justice and righteousness walk hand in hand, true liberation is achieved.

As we move forward, the Black Church must continue to navigate the delicate balance of faith and activism, ensuring that it remains faithful to the Gospel while standing boldly for justice. In doing so, it will continue to fulfill its role as a beacon of hope, a pillar of truth, and a catalyst for righteous transformation in the world.

6

Worship, Preaching, and the Spirit

Worship, preaching, and the movement of the Holy Spirit have always been central to the life of the Black Church. These elements not only shape the identity of Black Christianity but also serve as spiritual and communal expressions of faith. In the midst of slavery, segregation, and systemic oppression, the Black Church cultivated a worship tradition that was vibrant, soul-stirring, and deeply rooted in biblical truth. Preaching became a prophetic voice that guided, encouraged, and convicted its hearers, while the Holy Spirit's presence brought transformation, empowerment, and resilience to the community of believers.

This chapter will explore the theological foundation of worship in the Black Church, the power of preaching as an instrument of faith and social change, and the role of the Holy Spirit in sustaining and energizing Black Christians throughout history.

The Theology of Worship in the Black Church

Worship in the Black Church is more than mere ritual or tradition; it is a sacred encounter with God. From the sorrow songs of the enslaved to the contemporary gospel anthems that fill sanctuaries today, Black worship has always been an act of both spiritual devotion and resistance.

John 4:24 (KJV) declares, *"God is a Spirit: and they that worship him must worship him in spirit and in truth."* This verse reflects the heart of Black worship—an experience that engages both the emotions and the intellect, the personal and the communal. Worship in the Black Church is an act of survival, renewal, and transformation. Whether through song, prayer, or testimony, it reflects the deep faith of a people who have endured trials but remain steadfast in their hope in God.

Music, in particular, plays an integral role in worship. Negro spirituals, gospel hymns, and contemporary praise songs serve as vehicles of theological expression and collective memory. The call-and-response tradition within Black worship mirrors biblical patterns of communal participation in praise, as seen in Psalm 136, where the congregation responds in unison, affirming the faithfulness of God.

Preaching as a Prophetic and Transformative Force

Preaching in the Black Church has historically been a powerful tool for both spiritual instruction and social critique. Rooted in the biblical tradition of the prophets, Black preachers have proclaimed messages that call people to righteousness while addressing injustices in the world around them.

Romans 10:14 (KJV) asks, *"How then shall they call on him in whom they have not believed? and how shall they believe in him of whom they have not heard? and how shall they hear without a preacher?"* This verse underscores the necessity of preaching in bringing people to faith and inspiring them to action.

From the early days of plantation churches, where enslaved ministers preached in hush harbors, to the thunderous sermons of the Civil Rights Movement, Black preaching has always been marked by passion, conviction, and biblical depth. Sermons in the Black Church are not merely educational; they are encounters with the living Word, designed to uplift, convict, and mobilize listeners.

The Role of the Holy Spirit in the Black Church

The Holy Spirit is at the heart of Black worship and preaching. The movement of the Spirit brings liberation, healing, and empowerment, allowing believers to endure suffering while remaining hopeful for victory.

Acts 1:8 (KJV) affirms, *"But ye shall receive power, after that the Holy Ghost is come upon you: and ye shall be witnesses unto me both in Jerusalem, and in all Judaea, and in Samaria, and unto the uttermost part of the earth."* This verse highlights the Spirit's role in empowering believers to be bold witnesses for Christ.

The Black Church has always emphasized the active presence of the Holy Spirit in personal and corporate worship. The emotional expressions of faith—shouting, dancing, and speaking in tongues—are reflections of a deep spiritual connection with God. The Spirit not only comforts and strengthens believers but also emboldens them to challenge injustice and stand firm in their convictions.

Apologetic Defense: Answering the Critics

Some critics argue that the expressive nature of Black worship is excessive or purely emotional, lacking theological depth. However, biblical worship has always included dynamic expressions of praise, from David's dancing before the Lord (2 Samuel 6:14) to the joyful proclamations of the early Church. The vibrancy of Black worship is not a distraction but a demonstration of heartfelt devotion and faith.

Others claim that Black preaching is too focused on social justice rather than biblical doctrine. While it is true that Black preaching has historically addressed issues of oppression and inequality, it has never done so at the expense of sound doctrine. The prophetic tradition of preaching found in the Black Church aligns with Scripture's call to advocate for righteousness and justice (Amos 5:24).

Lastly, some question the emphasis on the Holy Spirit in the Black Church, suggesting that emotionalism is mistaken for genuine spirituality. However, Scripture makes it clear that the Spirit moves in powerful and tangible ways (1 Corinthians 2:4-5). The manifestations of the Spirit in the Black Church reflect a biblically sound engagement with God's presence and power.

Conclusion
Worship, preaching, and the movement of the Holy Spirit are central to the identity and vitality of the Black Church. These elements sustain believers in times of hardship, inspire them to live out their faith boldly, and create a communal experience that reflects the glory of God. The Black Church's expressions of faith are deeply biblical, historically significant, and spiritually transformative.

As we continue forward, the Black Church must remain rooted in these expressions, ensuring that worship is sincere, preaching remains prophetic, and the Spirit is welcomed to move freely. In doing so, it will continue to serve as a sanctuary for souls, a training ground for disciples, and a beacon of hope for future generations.

Defending the Faith in a Changing World

7

Answering the Critics

Throughout history, the Black Church has been both a beacon of hope and a target of criticism. While its contributions to social justice, theological thought, and spiritual formation are undeniable, it has also faced scrutiny from within and outside the faith. Some argue that the Black Church is too emotional in its worship, too focused on justice over doctrine, or too rooted in the past to be relevant in contemporary Christianity. Others claim that Christianity itself is a tool of oppression that the Black Church should abandon.

This chapter will address these critiques head-on, offering a deeper insight into these concerns rather than reiterating what was already discussed in Chapter 1. By referencing prior discussions and expanding on the theological and historical foundations of the Black Church, we will reaffirm its relevance and necessity in today's world.

Is Christianity a White Man's Religion?
As discussed in Chapter 1, Christianity's roots in Africa are undeniable. Rather than rehashing the early presence of Christianity on the continent, we must now ask: Why does this critique persist despite historical evidence to the contrary? One reason is the weaponization of Christianity by colonial and slaveholding powers, who distorted

the Gospel for their own benefit. However, recognizing this misuse does not invalidate Christianity itself.

The Black Church has responded to this critique by reclaiming and reshaping Christianity in a way that aligns with biblical truth and historical reality. Rather than viewing Christianity as a foreign imposition, Black theologians and preachers have emphasized its liberating message, drawing parallels between the biblical Exodus and the struggles of Black people in America. By understanding Christianity through the lens of faithfulness rather than colonial manipulation, the Black Church has preserved its identity as a faith of deliverance, not domination. Rejecting Christianity because of its misuse by oppressors would be akin to rejecting democracy or education because of their historical distortions. The question should not be whether Christianity was misused, but whether its true message aligns with the liberation of the oppressed—and history and Scripture affirm that it does.

Is the Black Church Too Emotional?
One of the most common critiques of the Black Church is that its worship style is overly emotional, with expressions such as shouting, dancing, and call-and-response preaching being perceived as excessive or lacking theological depth. However, worship in the Black Church is deeply rooted in both biblical tradition and the lived experience of a people who have endured suffering yet found hope in God. Emotional engagement in worship is not a distraction but a powerful affirmation of faith, resilience, and gratitude.

Faith in the Black Church is not merely intellectual; it is experiential. Theologians often refer to the Black Church's worship as an embodiment of lived theology—one where emotions are not suppressed but fully embraced as a way of encountering God. Expressive worship is not disorderly but a communal way of engaging with the divine, much like David's exuberant praise before the Ark of the Covenant (2 Samuel 6:14, KJV) or the early Church's passionate worship at Pentecost (Acts 2:1-4, KJV). The emotional depth of Black worship is an acknowledgment that God is present in both the joys and struggles of life.

Critics sometimes mistake this expressiveness for a lack of theological depth, but this assumption fails to recognize the robust preaching and doctrinal grounding that accompanies worship in the Black Church. Many of the most influential Black theologians and preachers—such as Richard Allen, Charles Tindley, and Gardner C. Taylor—infused their deeply biblical sermons with passion and conviction. Emotion in worship does not replace intellectual engagement; it enhances it. Just as music, art, and poetry can elevate understanding, so too does passionate worship deepen one's relationship with God.

Furthermore, the joy expressed in worship is an act of defiance against oppression, a declaration that despite historical suffering, Black believers choose to rejoice in the Lord (Philippians 4:4, KJV). Worship in the Black Church is not an escape from reality but a divine encounter that provides strength for life's challenges. It is a reminder that even in the darkest times, God is worthy of praise, and faith remains unshaken. Thus, far from being a weakness, the emotional nature of Black worship is one of its greatest strengths, anchoring believers in an unbreakable connection with God.

Is the Black Church Too Focused on Social Justice?

As previously addressed in Chapter 5, the Black Church's commitment to justice is not a distraction from the Gospel but an extension of it. Here, we delve deeper into the theological implications of this commitment.

Critics who claim that the Black Church has overemphasized justice at the expense of the Gospel often misunderstand the holistic nature of biblical faith. The Gospel is not only about personal salvation; it is about the transformation of individuals and communities. The call to justice is deeply embedded in Scripture, from the prophetic cries of Amos (Amos 5:24, KJV) to Jesus' own declaration in Luke 4:18-19 (KJV). The Black Church, in its advocacy for justice, has been faithfully living out the Gospel rather than distorting it.

Furthermore, history has shown that the Black Church's engagement in social justice has always been coupled with spiritual renewal. The Civil Rights Movement, for example, was not merely a political struggle—it was a spiritual movement, with prayer, fasting, and biblical teaching at its core. Social justice and spiritual formation are not competing forces but complementary ones, working together to fulfill God's will on earth.

Is the Black Church Stuck in Tradition?
While Chapter 6 addressed the historical significance of Black Church traditions, we now explore how tradition can be both a strength and a challenge in the modern era.

Tradition provides continuity, cultural identity, and a theological anchor. The Black Church's traditions—whether found in its style of worship, its organizational structure, or its communal focus—are not accidental but intentional, shaped by centuries of faith and perseverance. These traditions have sustained Black Christians through slavery, segregation, and systemic racism, offering a spiritual and cultural home where resilience and hope are cultivated.

However, like all Christian institutions, the Black Church must also engage with contemporary challenges. Tradition should serve as a foundation, not a limitation. While some churches struggle to engage younger generations, others have successfully adapted by incorporating digital ministries, contemporary worship styles, and new theological discussions while remaining rooted in Scripture. The key is not to abandon tradition but to ensure that it remains relevant and accessible, allowing the Black Church to maintain its prophetic voice in the ever-changing landscape of faith and culture.

Apologetic Defense: Answering the Critics

The critiques of the Black Church often arise from misunderstandings or misrepresentations of its theology and practice. Addressing these concerns requires a nuanced defense that acknowledges the Church's historical and theological significance.

One of the most common misconceptions is that Christianity is a tool of oppression, forced upon Black people through colonialism and slavery. However, as previously discussed, Christianity has deep African roots, and the Black Church has historically reclaimed the faith as a source of empowerment rather than subjugation. The Gospel message itself stands against oppression, offering liberation and hope to those who suffer. The Black Church, rather than being an agent of oppression, has served as a refuge for those seeking justice, dignity, and equality.

Another critique is that expressive worship in the Black Church is a distraction from sound doctrine. However, Scripture repeatedly affirms the role of emotional and physical expressions in worship. From David dancing before the Lord (2 Samuel 6:14) to the early Church's dynamic worship during Pentecost (Acts 2:1-4), the Bible shows that fervent worship is not a departure from faith but a demonstration of it. The Black Church's worship style reflects a deep spiritual engagement that brings both personal and communal renewal.

Some argue that the Black Church's focus on social justice overshadows the Gospel. However, justice is not an addition to the Gospel—it is a core aspect of biblical faith. The prophets consistently spoke against injustice, and Jesus Himself declared His mission to include liberating the oppressed (Luke 4:18-19). The Black Church has not replaced salvation with activism but has understood justice as an expression of true faith, aligning with James 2:26 (KJV): *"For as the body without the spirit is dead, so faith without works is dead also."*

Finally, critics claim that the Black Church is bound by tradition and resistant to change. While it is true that the Black Church values its rich heritage, this does not mean it is stagnant. The Church has continuously adapted to cultural shifts, integrating digital ministries, contemporary gospel music, and new theological perspectives while remaining rooted in Scripture. Tradition is not an obstacle; it is a foundation that provides continuity and identity while allowing for growth and renewal.

The Black Church remains a powerful force in Christianity, defending the faith, uplifting communities, and standing for justice. By addressing these critiques with biblical, historical, and theological clarity, it is evident that the Black Church is not a relic of the past but a living, evolving testimony to the enduring power of the Gospel.

Conclusion

The Black Church has endured centuries of criticism while remaining a pillar of faith, justice, and cultural identity. By addressing these critiques with theological depth and historical insight, we reaffirm that the Black Church is not an outdated institution but a vital force in Christianity today.

Rather than bending to external pressures or abandoning its mission, the Black Church must continue to stand firm in its convictions.

It must embrace both tradition and innovation, ensuring that it remains a source of spiritual strength for future generations. The legacy of the Black Church is one of resilience, resistance, and unwavering faith—and that legacy must continue to shine as a testament to the unchanging power of the Gospel.

8

The Black Church in a Digital Age

The Black Church has always been an evolving institution, adapting to cultural shifts while remaining rooted in biblical truth. In today's digital age, new challenges threaten to redefine faith, particularly with the rise of misinformation on social media, alternative Black spiritual movements, and a younger generation that is more skeptical of organized religion. However, these challenges also present opportunities for the Black Church to reaffirm its commitment to apologetics, discipleship, and evangelism.

This chapter explores how the Black Church must contend for the faith in an era where truth is often distorted, alternative belief systems challenge biblical authority, and digital engagement is crucial for reaching the next generation.

Social Media and Modern Challenges to Biblical Truth

Social media has revolutionized how information is shared, but it has also created an environment where biblical truth is frequently challenged. Misinformation about Christianity, historical distortions, and secular ideologies that conflict with Scripture are widespread across digital platforms. The Black Church must respond by equipping believers with sound doctrine and the ability to discern truth from falsehood.

One of the biggest concerns is the spread of "feel-good theology," which prioritizes self-empowerment over biblical obedience. Many influencers use platforms like TikTok, Instagram, and YouTube to promote a Christianity that is detached from accountability, repentance, and sound doctrine. The result is a generation exposed to spiritual half-truths that distort the message of Christ.

To counteract this, the Black Church must embrace digital apologetics—using social media, podcasts, and online content to educate and defend the faith. Just as Paul wrote letters to churches in the early Church era, today's ministers and theologians must use digital platforms to reinforce biblical literacy.

Additionally, pastors and church leaders must be proactive in discussing these challenges from the pulpit, ensuring that congregants are aware of the dangers of distorted theology and encouraging them to engage critically with what they consume online.

The Rise of Alternative Black Spiritual Movements

In recent decades, there has been a resurgence of alternative spiritual movements that challenge Christianity's place in Black identity. Movements such as African Traditional Religions (ATRs), the Black Hebrew Israelites, Kemetic spirituality, and Afrocentric humanism have gained popularity, particularly among younger Black individuals who question the historical role of Christianity in colonialism and slavery.

Many of these movements claim to offer a more "authentic" spiritual identity for Black people, arguing that Christianity is a European construct. However, as previously discussed, Christianity was present in Africa long before European colonization, and Black theologians have played a vital role in shaping Christian thought throughout history. The challenge for the Black Church is to address these misconceptions without alienating those who are drawn to these spiritual movements.

Rather than dismiss these movements outright, the Black Church must engage in meaningful dialogue. Apologetics must include historical education on the deep African roots of Christianity, the role of early African Church fathers, and the ways in which Christianity has been a force of liberation rather than oppression. Church leaders must be prepared to answer questions about Christianity's historical misuses while reaffirming the truth of the Gospel.

Furthermore, the Black Church must show how Christianity speaks to the very concerns that draw people to these alternative movements—identity, justice, and empowerment. The biblical message of redemption, liberation, and dignity in Christ must be emphasized to demonstrate that the faith of our ancestors is still relevant today.

Engaging the Next Generation with Apologetics

Many Millennials and Gen Zers are skeptical of organized religion, often questioning the validity of Christianity in a world where science, logic, and personal autonomy are highly valued. To engage this generation, the Black Church must make apologetics a priority—defending the faith with reason, historical evidence, and biblical truth.

One of the main reasons young people disengage from the Church is a lack of answers to tough questions. Topics such as the problem of evil, biblical reliability, racial justice, and Christianity's historical relationship with slavery must be addressed head-on. If the Church does not provide these answers, young people will turn to alternative sources that may misrepresent the truth.

Churches should consider incorporating apologetics courses, hosting Q&A sessions, and fostering open discussions where young people feel safe to ask difficult questions without fear of judgment. Additionally, mentoring relationships between older believers and younger generations can create spaces for discipleship and faith formation.

Engaging the next generation also requires a shift in how the Gospel is communicated. While the message of Christ remains unchanged, the methods must evolve. Digital platforms, interactive Bible studies, and spaces where faith and culture intersect are essential for ensuring that Christianity remains relevant to younger audiences.

Apologetic Defense: Answering the Critics of the Black Church in a Digital Age

As the Black Church navigates the digital age, critics argue that it is losing its influence and that traditional forms of faith are becoming obsolete. However, the need for spiritual guidance, justice advocacy, and theological clarity has never been greater.

Some claim that the younger generation is abandoning the Church altogether, but studies show that many young people are still spiritually curious—they simply reject institutionalized forms of religion that fail to engage them meaningfully. The challenge is not to water down Christianity but to create spaces where difficult conversations can take place while upholding biblical truth.

Others argue that digital ministry cannot replace in-person fellowship. While this is true, the Black Church must recognize that technology is a tool rather than a threat. The early Church used letters, oral tradition, and public gatherings to spread the Gospel; today, we have digital platforms that can accomplish the same mission on a global scale.

Finally, some critics suggest that engaging in apologetics and digital outreach compromises the traditional values of the Church. However, 1 Peter 3:15 (KJV) instructs believers to *"be ready always to give an answer to every man that asketh you a reason of the hope that is in you with meekness and fear."* The Black Church is called to defend the faith in every generation, using every available means to do so.

Conclusion

The Black Church's role in contending for the faith in the digital age is both a challenge and an opportunity. By confronting misinformation, engaging with alternative spiritual movements, and prioritizing apologetics for the next generation, it can ensure that biblical truth remains at the forefront.

As society changes, the Church must adapt its methods while remaining rooted in the unchanging Gospel. The call to contend for the faith requires wisdom, strategy, and courage. Just as the Black Church has historically been a beacon of hope and resistance, it must now rise to meet the challenges of the digital age, equipping believers to stand firm in their faith and share the Gospel with boldness and clarity.

9

Returning to Our First Love

Throughout its history, the Black Church has been a powerful force for spiritual renewal, justice, and community transformation. However, in recent years, many churches have faced challenges such as declining attendance, generational disengagement, and struggles to remain relevant in an ever-changing world. Despite these difficulties, the way forward lies not in abandoning the Church's foundation but in returning to its first love—Jesus Christ.

Revitalizing the Black Church today requires a renewed commitment to biblical discipleship, authentic worship, community engagement, and Spirit-led transformation. By reclaiming its mission, the Black Church can continue to thrive as a beacon of hope and faith for future generations.

Strengthening Biblical Literacy in the Black Church

A critical component of revitalization is a renewed commitment to biblical literacy. Many believers today struggle with a shallow understanding of Scripture, which can lead to spiritual stagnation and susceptibility to false teachings. Hosea 4:6 (KJV) warns, *"My people are destroyed for lack of knowledge."* To combat this, the Black Church must prioritize teaching sound doctrine and equipping believers with the tools to rightly divide the Word of Truth (2 Timothy 2:15, KJV).

Strengthening biblical literacy requires a multifaceted approach. Churches must invest in structured Bible study programs, theological education, and apologetics training that empower believers to defend their faith. Sunday School, midweek Bible classes, and mentorship programs should be reemphasized to ensure that both new and seasoned believers grow in their understanding of Scripture. Additionally, embracing digital resources, such as online Bible courses and interactive apps, can make biblical learning more accessible to younger generations.

When believers have a firm grasp of Scripture, they are better equipped to navigate life's challenges, resist cultural distortions of faith, and boldly share the Gospel with confidence. Strengthening biblical literacy will ensure that the Black Church remains rooted in God's Word, capable of addressing both spiritual and societal issues with clarity and authority.

The Role of Discipleship and Mentorship

A crucial aspect of revitalization is restoring the role of discipleship and mentorship within the Black Church. Discipleship is not simply about attending services—it is about spiritual growth, accountability, and training believers to become fully devoted followers of Christ. Jesus' model of discipleship was relational, intentional, and transformative, a model the Black Church must re-emphasize today.

Discipleship should be prioritized in both formal and informal settings. Structured Bible studies, small groups, and leadership training can help cultivate mature believers. At the same time, mentorship must be encouraged, where seasoned believers walk alongside younger Christians to provide guidance, encouragement, and biblical wisdom.

Titus 2:3-5 (KJV) emphasizes the importance of spiritual mentorship: *"The aged women likewise, that they be in behaviour as becometh holiness... That they may teach the young women to be sober, to love their husbands, to love their children."* Likewise, Paul's mentoring relationship with Timothy (2 Timothy 2:2, KJV) serves as a blueprint for strengthening the faith of new generations.

By prioritizing discipleship and mentorship, the Black Church can ensure that believers are not only spiritually mature but also equipped to lead and serve in their communities with boldness and conviction.

Restoring Authentic Worship and Prayer

Authentic worship is at the heart of the Black Church's identity. Throughout history, worship has been a source of strength, resilience, and renewal. However, in many cases, worship has become more about performance than encountering the presence of God.

John 4:24 (KJV) reminds us, *"God is a Spirit: and they that worship him must worship him in spirit and in truth."* The revitalization of the Black Church must begin with a return to worship that is Spirit-led, Christ-centered, and transformative. This means fostering environments where worship is not about entertainment but about a deep connection with God through prayer, praise, and surrender.

Prayer must also be restored as a foundational practice. Churches must become places of intercession, where believers regularly come together to seek God's face for personal renewal and community revival. When the Church prioritizes prayer, it invites divine power to transform hearts and minds.

Keeping the Focus on Jesus While Addressing Social Justice

The Black Church has historically been at the forefront of the fight for justice, advocating for the oppressed and standing against systemic injustices. However, as the Church continues this mission, it must be careful not to lose sight of its primary purpose: pointing people to Jesus Christ. Matthew 6:33 (KJV) reminds us, *"But seek ye first the kingdom of God, and his righteousness; and all these things shall be added unto you."* The pursuit of justice must be firmly rooted in the Gospel, ensuring that social activism does not overshadow the Church's call to proclaim salvation through Christ.

A Christ-centered approach to justice recognizes that true transformation begins in the heart. While addressing economic disparities, educational inequities, and systemic oppression is necessary, the Black Church must remain steadfast in preaching repentance, grace, and redemption through Jesus. Biblical justice is not merely about activism; it is about aligning society with God's moral law, as seen in Amos 5:24 (KJV): *"But let judgment run down as waters, and righteousness as a mighty stream."*

To maintain this balance, the Black Church must integrate the Gospel into its justice efforts. Whether feeding the hungry, advocating for policy changes, or mentoring at-risk youth, the goal must always be to reflect Christ's love and lead others to Him. This ensures that justice work remains a vehicle for Kingdom advancement rather than merely a social movement. When the Church keeps Jesus at the center, it can effectively engage in justice while fulfilling its spiritual mandate.

Apologetic Defense: Addressing the Need for Revival

Some critics argue that the Black Church is beyond revitalization, that its influence is fading, and that it has become disconnected from the needs of modern believers. However, history proves that the Black Church has always been a place of renewal and resurgence. Every major movement of spiritual revival in the Black Church—from the

Great Awakenings to the Civil Rights era—has emerged from a return to biblical truth, worship, and community service.

Others suggest that the Black Church has become too institutionalized, prioritizing traditions over spiritual growth. While tradition has its place, true revival comes when churches refocus on their mission—preaching Christ, making disciples, and serving the least among us.

Additionally, some claim that younger generations are no longer interested in church. However, studies show that many young people are still deeply spiritual; they are simply seeking a faith community that is authentic, engaged, and relevant. The Black Church must rise to the occasion by providing spaces where young people can wrestle with faith, ask tough questions, and experience God's transformative power.

Conclusion
The revitalization of the Black Church is not an impossible task—it is a necessary calling. By returning to its first love—Jesus Christ—the Church can reclaim its mission, strengthen its foundation, and continue to be a light in a dark world.

This renewal will require a deep commitment to discipleship, authentic worship, community engagement, and a willingness to adapt without compromising biblical truth. The God who sustained the Black Church through slavery, segregation, and systemic oppression is the same God who will empower its renewal today.

Now is the time for the Black Church to rise again, not just as an institution but as a movement of faith, love, and transformation. The future of the Black Church depends on its willingness to return to the heart of its calling—preaching Christ, making disciples, and serving as a beacon of hope for generations to come.

Marching On Till Victory Is Won

10

Marching On Till Victory Is Won

The Black Church has stood as a pillar of faith, endurance, and transformation for centuries. Rooted in the unshakable foundation of Jesus Christ, it has weathered the storms of slavery, segregation, systemic injustice, and societal shifts. Yet, despite the challenges, the Black Church continues to march forward—undaunted, unbowed, and unwavering. As we conclude this work, it is imperative to look ahead, reaffirming our commitment to faith, justice, discipleship, and the unchanging Gospel. The work is not done, and the journey is not over. We march on till victory is won.

The Black Church's Enduring Mission

Throughout history, the Black Church has been more than just a place of worship; it has been a movement. From the hush harbors of the enslaved to the pulpits of the Civil Rights Movement, it has declared the liberating power of the Gospel. Today, its mission remains the same: to exalt Christ, make disciples, serve the community, and be a prophetic voice against injustice.

The challenge in our current age is to maintain this mission with clarity and conviction. The Black Church cannot afford to drift into cultural complacency or allow secular ideologies to redefine its purpose. It must remain the salt and light that Jesus commanded it to be (Matthew 5:13-16, KJV). This means continuing to preach the uncompromising Gospel, equipping believers to live out their faith boldly, and ensuring that the Church remains a refuge for the weary and a training ground for disciples.

A key component of the Church's enduring mission is its role in shaping identity and faith within the Black community. For centuries, the Church has been the center of not only spiritual life but also cultural preservation, educational empowerment, and social justice advocacy. The Black Church must continue to bridge the gap between spiritual formation and societal transformation, ensuring that faith informs action, and action reflects faith. It must be a place where sound theology meets lived experience, where believers are both inspired and equipped to stand firm in their convictions.

As culture shifts and new ideologies emerge, the Black Church's role as a moral and spiritual anchor becomes even more critical. It must resist the temptation to conform to societal trends that dilute biblical truth while remaining engaged in meaningful, Christ-centered dialogue with the world. The Church must continue to train and send out disciples who will carry the Gospel into every sphere of life—education, politics, media, and business—ensuring that the message of Christ remains an active force in shaping the future.

Persevering Through Modern Challenges

The world today presents new challenges that threaten to weaken the Church's influence. The rise of secularism, the spread of misinformation through digital media, and the redefinition of morality pose significant threats to biblical truth. Additionally, generational shifts have led many younger people to disengage from traditional church structures.

Yet, just as the Black Church has faced obstacles before and overcome them, it will do so again. The key to persevering lies in returning to its biblical foundation. As Paul wrote in Galatians 6:9 (KJV), *"And let us not be weary in well doing: for in due season we shall reap, if we faint not."* The Church must remain steadfast in the Word, unshaken by cultural tides, and committed to the mission God has given it.

One of the greatest challenges facing the Church today is the rise of relativism—the idea that truth is subjective and morality is fluid. This mindset is at odds with the Gospel, which presents absolute truth and unchanging moral standards. The Black Church must be intentional about teaching sound doctrine, training believers in apologetics, and preparing them to stand firm in a world that increasingly rejects biblical principles.

Additionally, technology and digital culture have drastically reshaped how people engage with faith. While social media and online platforms provide opportunities for outreach, they also expose believers to competing worldviews and misinformation that can lead to confusion. The Black Church must actively engage in digital discipleship, ensuring that truth is proclaimed in every space where misinformation seeks to take root. Churches that embrace technology as a tool rather than a threat will find themselves better equipped to reach younger generations and remain a relevant voice in a rapidly changing world.

Another modern challenge is the ongoing struggle for racial and social justice. The Black Church has historically been a beacon of hope and a leader in advocating for equity and righteousness. However, as conversations around justice become increasingly polarized, the

Church must be careful not to be co-opted by political ideologies that either diminish or distort its biblical mission. The Black Church must ensure that its pursuit of justice remains rooted in the Gospel—fighting against oppression while pointing people to the ultimate justice found in Christ.

The Black Church must also address the spiritual fatigue that many believers experience in an era of relentless crises, social unrest, and economic instability. The Church must be a sanctuary for renewal, offering rest and encouragement through worship, community, and prayer. By fostering a culture of spiritual resilience, the Black Church will empower believers to persevere, knowing that their labor in the Lord is not in vain (1 Corinthians 15:58, KJV).

Victory Through Christ

True victory is not measured by earthly success but by faithfulness to God's calling. The Black Church's greatest triumph is not in numbers, wealth, or status, but in its unwavering commitment to Christ and His unchanging Gospel.

Jude 3 (KJV) exhorts believers to *"earnestly contend for the faith which was once delivered unto the saints."* The Black Church must remain steadfast in defending biblical truth, proclaiming salvation through Jesus Christ, and standing firm against doctrines that seek to dilute the Gospel's power. In a world of shifting values, the Church must hold to the eternal truth of God's Word, refusing to compromise for cultural acceptance.

Revelation 2:10 (KJV) reminds us, *"Be thou faithful unto death, and I will give thee a crown of life."* The victory we seek is not merely social or political—it is spiritual and eternal. As the Church remains faithful to its calling, it will see lives transformed, communities restored, and generations impacted for Christ.

As we press forward, we take encouragement from Hebrews 12:1-2 (KJV): *"Wherefore seeing we also are compassed about with so great a cloud of witnesses, let us lay aside every weight, and the sin which doth so easily beset us, and let us run with patience the race that is set before us, Looking unto Jesus the author and finisher of our faith."* The journey ahead will have struggles, but with Christ as our guide, victory is assured. True victory is not measured by earthly success but by faithfulness to God's calling. The Black Church's greatest triumph is not in numbers, wealth, or status, but in its unwavering commitment to Christ and His Gospel.

Conclusion

The Black Church's story is not over. The same faith that sustained our ancestors sustains us now. The same Gospel that empowered past generations empowers us today. The same God who strengthened those who cried out in faith remains faithful to His people now.

As we march forward, we must remain faithful to the unchanging Gospel. No matter how society shifts, God's truth does not change. The message of salvation, redemption, and justice through Jesus Christ remains the foundation upon which we stand. Galatians 1:8 (KJV) warns, *"But though we, or an angel from heaven, preach any other gospel unto you than that which we have preached unto you, let him be accursed."* The Black Church must not waver but must continue to proclaim the Good News with conviction and clarity.

Now is the time for the Black Church to stand boldly, contending for the faith with wisdom and courage. We must reject complacency, resist compromise, and reaffirm that our mission is as relevant today as it was in generations past. Our ancestors sang of the "God of our weary years," and we declare with confidence that He is still the God of today. He has not changed. He has not abandoned us. He is still guiding His Church, strengthening His people, and calling us to faithfulness.

We march on, not in our strength, but in His. We march on, not for personal gain, but for the glory of God. We march on, knowing that the final victory belongs to the Lord. Let the Church rise with renewed strength, let the people of God stand firm, and let us continue the work until the day when our faith is made sight.

March on, till victory is won.

A Timeline of the Black Church's Historical Impact

Early African Christianity (1st - 7th Century)

- **c. 50-100 AD** – The Ethiopian eunuch (Acts 8:27-39) is baptized, marking one of the earliest recorded African converts to Christianity.
- **c. 180-254 AD** – Origen of Alexandria, one of the early Church Fathers, influences Christian theology.
- **c. 354-430 AD** – Augustine of Hippo, an African bishop and theologian, writes *Confessions* and *The City of God*, shaping Christian doctrine for centuries.
- **c. 5th - 7th Century** – The decline of Christian influence in North Africa due to Islamic expansion.

The Black Church in the Era of Slavery (17th - 19th Century)

- **1619** – The first African slaves arrive in Virginia; enslaved Africans begin practicing Christianity, often in secret.
- **1773** – The first known Black Baptist church is founded in Silver Bluff, South Carolina.
- **1787** – Richard Allen and Absalom Jones establish the Free African Society in Philadelphia, laying the foundation for independent Black Christian institutions.
- **1816** – Richard Allen founds the African Methodist Episcopal (AME) Church, the first independent Black denomination in America.
- **1831** – Nat Turner, a Black preacher, leads a slave rebellion in Virginia, highlighting the role of Christian faith in resistance movements.

The Black Church and Abolition (19th Century)

- **1840s** – Black churches become centers for abolitionist activism, providing refuge for escaping slaves via the Underground Railroad.
- **1865** – The Civil War ends, and Black churches expand dramatically as freedmen establish independent congregations.
- **1895** – The National Baptist Convention, USA, Inc., the largest Black Protestant denomination, is formed.

The Black Church and the Civil Rights Movement (20th Century)

- **1906** – The Azusa Street Revival, led by William J. Seymour, sparks the rise of Pentecostalism, influencing Black churches worldwide.
- **1955-1968** – The Black Church leads the Civil Rights Movement:
    - **1955** – Rosa Parks, a devout Christian, refuses to give up her seat on a bus, sparking the Montgomery Bus Boycott.
    - **1963** – Martin Luther King Jr., a Baptist minister, delivers his "I Have a Dream" speech.
    - **1965** – The Selma to Montgomery marches, led by clergy including John Lewis, push for voting rights legislation.
    - **1968** – Martin Luther King Jr. is assassinated; his legacy cements the Black Church's role in justice and activism.

The Black Church in the Late 20th and Early 21st Century

- **1980s-1990s** – The rise of prosperity gospel movements creates theological debates within Black churches.
- **2008** – The election of Barack Obama, a candidate with strong ties to the Black Church, brings renewed discussions on faith and politics.
- **2020** – The Black Church plays a major role in social justice movements, advocating for racial equality and voter mobilization.
- **Present** – The Black Church faces challenges such as declining membership among younger generations but continues to serve as a moral and spiritual leader.

Conclusion

The Black Church has consistently been a force for spiritual renewal, social justice, and cultural empowerment. From its early African roots to its role in modern movements, it remains a vital institution in the Black community, continuing to shape history through faith and action.

Key Figures in Black Christian History

Early African Christian Leaders

- **Origen of Alexandria (c. 185-254 AD)** – Influential early Christian theologian and scholar from North Africa who contributed significantly to biblical interpretation and apologetics.
- **Tertullian (c. 155-240 AD)** – North African theologian who introduced Latin terminology into Christian theology and defended the faith against heresy.
- **Cyprian of Carthage (c. 200-258 AD)** – Bishop of Carthage and an early advocate for Church unity and pastoral leadership.
- **Augustine of Hippo (354-430 AD)** – One of the most important Church Fathers, whose writings, including *Confessions* and *The City of God*, have shaped Christian thought for centuries.

Leaders in the Era of Slavery and Abolition

- **Richard Allen (1760-1831)** – Founder of the African Methodist Episcopal (AME) Church, the first independent Black denomination in the U.S.
- **Absalom Jones (1746-1818)** – Co-founder of the Free African Society and the first African American priest ordained in the Episcopal Church.
- **Lott Carey (1780-1828)** – Baptist minister and missionary who helped establish Christian missions in Liberia.
- **Nat Turner (1800-1831)** – Enslaved preacher who led a rebellion in Virginia, seeing his fight for freedom as divinely inspired.
- **Frederick Douglass (1818-1895)** – Former slave, abolitionist, and orator who frequently invoked Christian principles in his advocacy for freedom and justice.

Builders of the Black Church

- **Henry McNeal Turner (1834-1915)** – AME bishop, missionary, and advocate for African repatriation.
- **Charles Harrison Mason (1866-1961)** – Founder of the Church of God in Christ (COGIC), one of the largest Pentecostal denominations in the world.

- **William J. Seymour (1870-1922)** – Leader of the Azusa Street Revival, which helped spread Pentecostalism globally.
- **Nannie Helen Burroughs (1879-1961)** – Educator and women's rights advocate who founded the National Training School for Women and Girls and was active in the National Baptist Convention.
- **Garveyite Christian Leaders (1920s-1930s)** – Clergy members who aligned with Marcus Garvey's back-to-Africa movement while integrating Christian theology.

Theologians and Civil Rights Leaders

- **Howard Thurman (1899-1981)** – Theologian and mentor to Dr. Martin Luther King Jr., whose work emphasized nonviolent resistance and the mystical aspects of Christianity.
- **Martin Luther King Jr. (1929-1968)** – Baptist minister and civil rights leader who used Christian theology to advocate for justice and equality.
- **James H. Cone (1938-2018)** – Founder of Black Liberation Theology, emphasizing Christianity's role in the fight against racial injustice.
- **Gardner C. Taylor (1918-2015)** – Renowned Baptist preacher known as the "Dean of American Preaching."

Contemporary Leaders and Thinkers

- **Prathia Hall (1940-2002)** – Baptist preacher, theologian, and civil rights activist whose rhetoric influenced King's "I Have a Dream" speech.
- **C.T. Vivian (1924-2020)** – Baptist minister and key leader in the Civil Rights Movement.
- **Barbara A. Holmes (b. 1955)** – Theologian and scholar focusing on African American spirituality and social justice.
- **T.D. Jakes (b. 1957)** – Bishop of The Potter's House, influential pastor, and author.
- **Otis Moss III (b. 1970)** – Pastor and author known for his work in prophetic preaching and social justice.
- **Samuel C. Tolbert, Jr. (b. 1965)** – President of the National Baptist Convention of America, dedicated to church growth and leadership development.
- **Jeremiah Wright (b. 1941)** – Theologian and pastor emeritus of Trinity United Church of Christ, known for his advocacy of Black liberation theology.
- **Jesse Jackson (b. 1941)** – Baptist minister, civil rights leader, and founder of the Rainbow PUSH Coalition, a key figure in social justice and political activism.

Conclusion

These individuals represent the enduring faith, resilience, and influence of the Black Church. From early African theologians to modern-day leaders, they have shaped Christian thought, ministry, and social change in profound ways. Their legacies continue to inspire future generations to live out their faith boldly and impact the world for Christ.

Suggested Books and Resources for Further Reading

Historical Foundations of the Black Church

- Raboteau, Albert J. *Slave Religion: The "Invisible Institution" in the Antebellum South* – A foundational work on the spiritual lives of enslaved Africans in America.
- Lincoln, C. Eric, and Lawrence H. Mamiya. *The Black Church in the African American Experience* – A comprehensive study of the role of the Black Church in American history.
- Fulop, Timothy E., and Albert J. Raboteau, eds. *African-American Religion: Interpretive Essays in History and Culture* – A collection of scholarly essays on the historical development of Black Christianity.
- Johnson, Sylvester A. *African American Religions, 1500–2000: Colonialism, Democracy, and Freedom* – Explores the evolution of Black religious thought and practice over centuries.

Theology and Doctrine

- Cone, James H. *A Black Theology of Liberation* – A foundational text on Black Liberation Theology.
- Felder, Cain Hope, ed. *Stony the Road We Trod: African American Biblical Interpretation* – Examines biblical interpretation through the lens of African American experience.
- Thurman, Howard. *Jesus and the Disinherited* – A classic exploration of Jesus' teachings in the context of oppression and resistance.
- Evans, Tony. *Oneness Embraced: Reconciliation, the Kingdom, and How We are Stronger Together* – Addresses racial reconciliation and unity in the Church.
- McCaulley, Esau. *Reading While Black: African American Biblical Interpretation as an Exercise in Hope* – A fresh perspective on how the Black Church reads and applies Scripture.

Preaching and Worship in the Black Church

- Taylor, Gardner C. *The Words of Gardner Taylor* – A collection of sermons from one of the most influential preachers in Black Church history.
- Moss, Otis III. *Blue Note Preaching in a Post-Soul World: Finding Hope in an Age of Despair* – A theological and homiletical reflection on Black preaching traditions.
- Mitchell, Henry H. *Black Preaching: The Recovery of a Powerful Art* – An in-depth study on the history and method of Black preaching.
- Allen, Richard, and Sarah Allen. *The Life, Experience, and Gospel Labors of the Rt. Rev. Richard Allen* – Autobiographical writings from the founder of the AME Church.

Social Justice and the Black Church

- Baldwin, Lewis. *The Voice of Conscience: The Church in the Mind of Martin Luther King, Jr.* – Examines the theological underpinnings of King's activism.
- Glaude, Eddie S. Jr. *Exodus! Religion, Race, and Nation in Early Nineteenth-Century Black America* – Explores how Exodus theology shaped early Black American identity.
- West, Cornel. *Prophetic Fragments* – A theological critique of race, class, and justice.
- Tisby, Jemar. *The Color of Compromise: The Truth about the American Church's Complicity in Racism* – A historical and theological analysis of racism in the Church.
- Walker-Barnes, Chanequa. *I Bring the Voices of My People: A Womanist Vision for Racial Reconciliation* – A womanist theological perspective on race and faith.

Contemporary Issues in the Black Church

- Jakes, T.D. *Woman, Thou Art Loosed!* – A theological reflection on healing and restoration for women in the Church.
- Wright, Jeremiah A. *Africans Who Shaped Our Faith* – A study of African influence in biblical history.
- Moss, Otis III. *Dancing in the Darkness: Spiritual Lessons for Thriving in Turbulent Times* – Encouragement for faith amid contemporary struggles.
- Carter, J. Kameron. *Race: A Theological Account* – A theological discussion on race and Christianity.
- Walton, Jonathan L. *Watch This! The Ethics and Aesthetics of Black Televangelism* – A critique of modern Black televangelism.

Online Resources and Digital Platforms

- **The African American Lectionary** (www.theafricanamericanlectionary.org) – A resource for Black Church liturgy and worship planning.
- **The Samuel DeWitt Proctor Conference** (www.sdpconference.info) – A network of Black faith leaders working on social justice initiatives.
- **PBS Documentary: "The Black Church: This Is Our Story, This Is Our Song"** – A visual exploration of Black Church history and influence.
- **Howard University School of Divinity** – A leading institution for Black theological education.

Conclusion

These books and resources provide deeper insight into the history, theology, preaching, and social justice work of the Black Church. Whether for academic study, personal growth, or ministry development, these works help strengthen the foundation upon which the Black Church continues to stand.

Bibliography

The Holy Bible, King James Version (KJV).

Allen R. The Life, Experience, and Gospel Labors of the Rt. Rev. Richard Allen. Philadelphia: Martin & Boden; 1833.

Douglass F. Narrative of the Life of Frederick Douglass, an American Slave. Boston: Anti-Slavery Office; 1845.

King ML Jr. Strength to Love. New York: Harper & Row; 1963.

Turner HM. The Genius and Theory of Methodist Polity. Philadelphia: AME Book Concern; 1885.

Baldwin L. The Voice of Conscience: The Church in the Mind of Martin Luther King, Jr. Oxford: Oxford University Press; 2010.

Cone JH. A Black Theology of Liberation. New York: Orbis Books; 1970.

Felder CH, ed. Stony the Road We Trod: African American Biblical Interpretation. Minneapolis: Fortress Press; 1991.

Fulop TE, Raboteau AJ, eds. African-American Religion: Interpretive Essays in History and Culture. New York: Routledge; 1997.

Lincoln CE, Mamiya LH. The Black Church in the African American Experience. Durham: Duke University Press; 1990.

Raboteau AJ. Slave Religion: The "Invisible Institution" in the Antebellum South. Oxford: Oxford University Press; 2004.

Thurman H. Jesus and the Disinherited. Boston: Beacon Press; 1949.

Glaude ES Jr. Exodus! Religion, Race, and Nation in Early Nineteenth-Century Black America. Chicago: University of Chicago Press; 2000.

McCaulley E. Reading While Black: African American Biblical Interpretation as an Exercise in Hope. Downers Grove: IVP Academic; 2020.

Tisby J. The Color of Compromise: The Truth about the American Church's Complicity in Racism. Grand Rapids: Zondervan; 2019.

West C. Prophetic Fragments. Grand Rapids: Eerdmans; 1988.

Walton JL. Watch This! The Ethics and Aesthetics of Black Televangelism. New York: NYU Press; 2009.

Howard University School of Divinity. Black Theology and The Black Church. Washington, DC: Howard University Press; 2017.

Jakes TD. God's Leading Lady: Out of the Shadows and Into the Light. New York: Berkley; 2002.

Moss O III. Dancing in the Darkness: Spiritual Lessons for Thriving in Turbulent Times. New York: Simon & Schuster; 2022.

PBS Documentary. *The Black Church: This Is Our Story, This Is Our Song*. Directed by Henry Louis Gates Jr. PBS; 2021.

www.ingramcontent.com/pod-product-compliance
Lightning Source LLC
Chambersburg PA
CBHW060649030426
42337CB00017B/2527